God's Gift

Inspired by the Holy Spirit

JAMES D. DANIELS

ISBN 979-8-88943-305-7 (paperback)
ISBN 979-8-88943-306-4 (digital)

Christian Faith Publishing
832 Park Avenue
Meadville, PA 16335
www.christianfaithpublishing.com

Printed in the United States of America

Your Love

Your love is like a dove that shines like the first break of spring dew.
Spring dew
On the flower that you are. For what is put before you are angels all
around you
To guard and protect you from the evil of man, the light shines
bright, and even
Though it may dim from darkness, your love will always shine
through
For God so loves the world that He gave his only begotten son that
you may live
And shine in the light forever more.

Amen.

Old Man

There was an old man who had a jar, he knew it was a sin because the jar was full of gin

I told him about Christ and how his life could be, I was only three, and he said I once had

Two small children and a good wife, and now they are far from my life all mad and full of

Haste, he grabbed his jar and got into his car, he did not see that big oak tree, there he

Died, I was only three. But to my amaze, it was just a sight to see, just one small light that

Old man did not die, the heavens above gave him the great divine, that night that old

Man died to be born again, oh, what joy can you see in one in one small boy, I was only

Three.

Precious Lord

Precious Lord, take my hand, hold me tight so I understand
Precious Lord, take my hand, hold me tight throughout the night
And when I do not understand around his presence I will begin
So, precious Lord, take my hand, hold me tight throughout the night.

Darkness of My Mind

As I sit in this cell the darkness of this torture, no light to see darkness
will surely prevail over the cell
My mind in me the dark place, I will be as I sit day by day a small
light comes in to stay for the
Lord, heard my mom as she prayed day by day, my mom was there
to stay on her knees every
Day forever to stay the darkness the cell of my mind a light breaking
through as my mom pray
Time after time for me, and you so now as I let the Lord come
through the darkness the cell of my
Mind becoming bright for me and you time after time, the Lord
heard my mom as she prayed
On my knees every day forever to stay as I think of my mom
December, the Lord's birthday, the
Best gift she gave the Lord was me on my knees every day forever to
stay as He took my mom
Away on December day forever to stay

Amen.

Lord Makes Friends

My friend was my friend when I needed a friend
I was his friend when he needed a friend
Where was my friend
For my friend was to the end
So I ask my friend
Who was my friend
To be my friend
And he had a friend because I was his friend
He was my friend
So I knew I have a friend who is my friend
Friends to the end.

Knowing God

I come to you
Here to say
You need the Lord every day
The Lord is coming
You do not know what day
It's your life
He's here to say
The day you leave
I am here to say
The Lord is coming
That's the day
Look at yourself
Not at me
Look in the mirror
And what do you see
Its time now
For you to believe
The Lord is coming
You will see

Amen.

Jesus Loves You

When we go to hide
So angels on the outside
What we do
It's up to you
Angels will be there for you
The Lord gave us
A great divine
His very best
To guard and protect
In due time
You know the rest
Life past us by
By a wink of an eye
And you are old inside
Where is the Lord
You passed him by
So give him a chance
Bring him inside
At this point
Don't say goodbye
For every moment of every day
The Lord so dearly
Wants to stay

Amen.

Lord Jesus

You made the clouds
For me to see
Me and you to believe
In the only begotten son
That we may trust and believe
You wash the clouds
As your son Jesus
Wash our sins
To keep us pure in heart
I love you, Father God
For making a wretched person like me
Whole and clean

Amen.

Hurting Inside

Remember the day
I was arrogant
All full of pride
If anybody talks to me
About the Lord Jesus
I would laugh at them
But little did they know
I was hurting inside
For every time I did not like somebody
I did not know
I didn't like myself
How can I love myself
When I don't know how to be kind
The Lord is good
The Lord is great
That's how I know to get straight
But who is out there
To help a wretched fool like me
For long is the highway
That many people will follow
For my shallow mind is hollow
Someone told me the road to righteousness
Is a narrow road that many will follow
But only a few will find
So do as the Lord says
Be kind, love one another
And go the right way
Down that narrow road to righteousness
And do what you are told

Amen.

Me

Is it my imagination
Or is it real
I do believe
To have the fill
Of the Lord
Living inside of me
So it's time
To believe
In the only one
I can see
The Lord God
He's very good to me
Oh, can't you see
He lives inside of me

Amen.

Love

The storm of my life
Rages on as I choose to believe
In the one and only
That's inside of me
From good to evil
Which way do I go
Up or below
I do not know
So as I start my day
In prayer, I ask the Lord
To help me in every way
Nothing belongs to me
It's for the Lord
For now, I can see
And the only way
Is to believe
In the one and only
That is me

Amen.

The Love in Me

Who is there to see
If I love my friend in need
I say I love
But is there love
If I don't have it in me
How can you see the love
That's in thee
If the Lord is not there to be
So, Lord, strip my heart layer by layer
To be pure indeed
For when my friend asks in need
I will be there for him to see

Amen.

The Lord

I see the Lord painted
The clouds so white
For me to know he's in plain sight
And when the clouds turn dark and gray
It's time for me to pray
I know Satan is there for me that day
But I see a light that appears
Through the dark and gray clouds
For me to know it's the way for me to go
As the Lord will stay every day
So when I am empty and nowhere inside
I know the Lord is there
He will guide
With his light so bright
That's why he painted the clouds so white

Amen.

The Sign

Trust in the Lord
And you will find
If you wait on him
He will give you a sign
What to do every day
So on your knee
He expects you to pray
Not one time but every day
The Lord loves you dearly
Because He went to the cross
For me and you
We were bought
With a heavy price
So love your neighbor
And be kind
Because you were bought and that's a lot

Amen.

Life

Like the sand in your hand
Time by time passes you by
With the water in your hands
That dribbles through
Before you know it
You are two
From the younger you are
To the older you feel
Where are you what do you do
Nowhere to go or even to hide
For your life is in plain sight
Like the sand in your hand
With the water that dribbles through
Before you know it you are too

Amen.

Walked Away

You brought me up, and I let you down
Your life you gave me forever to stay
And I walked away
Please help me, for I want to stay
In your life forever to stay and ever and ever
Everyday your love I want the love you gave me
And do I really know that it is there
I pretend every day that it's alright
But it's me the love that I say
Really there every day
The love I show you
The love you give me
Sometimes I show you for it to be real
But is it, or is it not
Only I do believe with my heart
For I know you are not far
So I keep on doing the things I do
And I have always known it's you
Please keep giving me your love
Your kindness above
For all I ask is for all from above

Amen.

Believing

And when I fall
I fight again
For the freedom
God has given us
To live again
Love is great
Love is good
But if it's not in your heart
For God, that's no good
Come on, people
Where are you at
Stand up for the Lord
And that's that

Amen.

I am a poem writer
As you can see
My writing for you to believe
In the Lord Jesus every day
So as you look at my stuff
Remember the Holy Spirit
Gave it up

Amen.

About the Author

James Daniels is from Galveston, Texas and is happily married to his best friend, Crystal Daniels. He is a believer in Jesus Christ, who he says has inspired him to write these poems.

Printed in the USA
CPSIA information can be obtained
at www.ICGtesting.com
LVHW041814210124
769094LV00003B/475